TETHERS END

Tethers End

poems by
Jeanne Blum Lesinski

Shanti Arts Publishing
Brunswick, Maine

Tethers End

Copyright © 2023 Jeanne Blum Lesinski

All Rights Reserved
No part of this document may be reproduced or transmitted in any form or by any means without prior written permission of the publisher, except in the case of brief quotations embodied in critical reviews.

Published by Shanti Arts Publishing

Designed by Shanti Arts Designs

Cover image: Claude Monet, *Cliff Walk at Pourville*, 1882. Oil on canvas. 26 1/8 × 32 7/16 inches (66.5 × 82.3 cm). Art Institute of Chicago, Chicago, Illinois. Public domain.

Shanti Arts LLC
193 Hillside Road
Brunswick, Maine 04011
shantiarts.com

Printed in the United States of America

ISBN: 978-1-962082-08-2 (softcover)

Library of Congress Control Number: 2023947901

To the Ones I Love

Contents

Acknowledgments ... 9

Review	11
Flight	12
Father's Flannel	13
The Dune	14
Black and White	16
Die Bibliothekarin: A Sestina	18
Recipe Box	20
Daily Drag	22
Thirst	23
Re: ER	24
Autopsy Retort	26
Wild Must Be Wild	28
Into Blue	29
Paradigm Shift	30
Heart in My Garden	31
3:30 a.m.	32
Mid-January Snow	33
Analogies	34
Lot	36
Hydrology of Tears	38
Tether's End	39
Dresden Plate	40
Mousery	41
False Crocus Geometer	42
Bruised, Not Broken	43
Window Washer	44
My Perfect Cup of Coffee	45
Picky Eater	46
Tonic	49
Hardware	50
Signs of Character	51
At the Y	52
Heave	53
World in Motion	54
Bear-Garden	56
Personal Pompeii	57
I Believe in Silence (of a sort)	58
Declaration	61
Some Things Shift	62
Geodes	64
Final Proof	66

About the Author ... 69

Acknowledgments

Grateful acknowledgment is made to the editors of the following publications in which these poems first appeared, sometimes in slightly different form:

Binnacle (Ultra-Short Competition): "Personal Pompeii"
Book of Matches: "Into Blue"
CaKe: "At the Y"
Cardinal Sins: "Bruised, Not Broken"; "Paradigm Shift"; and "Tonic"
Cherry Blossom Review: "Window Washer"
deLuge: "Picky Eater—Benefits of Being Dull" and "Picky Eater—Why We [Cook]"
Drash: "Hydrology of Tears"
The Dunes Review: "False Crocus Geometer"; "My Perfect Cup of Coffee"; "Review"; and "Thirst"
Ginosko: "Flight"
Goose River Press Anthology: "Recipe Box"
The Kitchen Sink Magazine: "Autopsy Retort"
Kudzu: "Father's Flannel"
Last Leaves Leaving: "Dresden Plate"
Montana State University's Read This: "Die Bibliothekarin: A Sestina" and "Re: ER"
Pennsylvania English: "Black and White"; "The Dune"; and "Heart in My Garden"
Plainsongs: "World in Motion"
The Tarwolf Review: "Tether's End

Review

Intersects, accidental meetings jar
my reason—on I-80 no man's land
a college colleague's friendship to renew,
a transatlantic meeting at IU,
a Sunday morning motorcycle (pole-
obscured, one-second glance) collision, roll—
confirm my blinders, *im*-perception, "view."
I watch the monarch larva change by far
from caterpillar (striped green, yellow and
black) to cocoon in seconds: thirty-two.

Flight

We wander along the dune crest, following meandering sand lines, wave markers; little holes, once bubbles speckle the dune's lake side. With our bared feet the same size, we leave almost matching footprints, dry colored ones on the dark sand, wet-colored ones on the dry. Further inland the dunes rise up, a gentle clutter of congregating grass. Our loose sweatshirts and jeans, rolled up to mid-calf, flap wildly. The autumn breeze combs our hair, caresses our faces, fills our nostrils with the scent of clean sand, fresh, clear water, pushes the massed, gray-tinged clouds in streams across the reflected sky. The great green-blue lake lashes roaring three-foot waves. We dodge them easily laughing, as they lap at our ankles. Stripe-necked sandpipers scatter on chopstick legs, leaving mazes. Herring gulls swirl above, glide through invisible dance patterns, dip abruptly to light amidst the foamy waves. We open our flapping sails to the breeze to take it all in, to pour ourselves all out, to become grains of sand underfoot, crystal jewels of sparkling foam, almost imperceptible whirs of gulls' wings.

Father's Flannel

Though monochrome, the photo colors bright
the unadulterated joy of my small dimple,
pressed to his, in warm delight.

His strong plaid flanneled arms encircle me
with love so rich, deep, yet ever light,
give me sure knowledge of eternity.

Shirts, night gowns, pajamas, all flannel, they
hold magic that by fleece cannot be worn,
nor can the quick, passing years wear away.

Three decades from the camera's eye, so too,
my toddler's take-along becomes for me,
no dust cloth, but a flannel memory.

The Dune

The weathered gray barn squats
between elm grove and sawmill,
where Grandfather brings to life
the monstrous, jagged-toothed saw,
its steely blade my height.

Like the toothpicks of some Bunyan,
the pine trunks await their fate,
at each end weeping amber sap,
trapping would-be scarabs,
and my anticipation.

Watching for Grandmother, I jump—
faded overalls, sky blue blouse,
huckleberry buckets in hand—
as the saw motor starts,
sputters, then growls steadily.

Rattling chains draw logs
to the first of many snarling bites.
Blond chips and dust fly,
settling like resinous sand,
in a pile behind the mill.

Silently the dune beckons
like a Michigan shore
on a sticky August afternoon.
I wade to the top, slide down again
and again in an avalanche

of slivers, until finally,
ready to meet blueberries,
I empty pant cuffs, shake pigtails.
Only the barn notices the slap-and-dash
as I mill the evidence of my trespass.

Black and White

At the outskirts of town,
the black-and-white sign reads:
"Fourth largest Amish community
in the nation." On Main Street,
a horse trots, pulling a black buggy.

A bearded face peers ahead,
while his weathered hands dance the reins.
A toddler perches on his mother's lap,
clutches a Sparkle bag of corn chips,
waves a chubby hand at me, a Yankee.

Over the hill crest careen skaters
in Granny Smith green dresses.
White bonnet ties flying,
they race past schoolhouse,
woodpile, privies.

In straw hats, suspended blue pants,
with Igloo-cooler lunch pails dangling,
aluminum baseball bats slung over shoulders,
Amish schoolboys talk box scores
as they trudge home to chores.

On lines from white house
to carriage barn, to maple,
teal, maroon, violet polyester dresses
wave long sleeves and skirts,
like unpieced quilts.

Nutmeg Belgians pull plows
across stubborn corn stubble,
while on steep ditch slopes
men wielding gas-powered Weedwackers
cut quick swathes.

At Yoder and Miller farms,
aboard a rainbow-sided Bookmobile,
deutsch-chattering girls, proud
mothers at sixteen, check out
romances by the bag full.
After midnight hooves clatter.
A beer bottle crashes
in the derelict churchyard,
where once an Amishman
hid his forbidden automobile.

When sons or daughters Yank over,
do parents cease loving them?
In my mother's heart,
I somehow know
their black-and-white life is not.

Die Bibliothekarin: A Sestina

About the stacks I weave my check-out cart,
pause, ponder, do my part, fill every bag
with fiction, magazines, and picture books,
all destined for my Amish patrons, when
at their farmhouses, bags in hand, I will light
to visit *Kinder, Frauen* for a while.
Anticipation rises in me while
I check out and bag each book, load, and cart
them to my waiting car. They are not light—
these canvas sacks hold more than words. Each bag
contains a glimpse of the wide-spread world. When
I go to their doors, *Kinder* grab their books.
They *danke* me and run off with the books
clasped firmly in chubby fists, run off while
with *Mutter* I chat (gardens, quilts, jams), when
"Ach, look!" says *Bruder*, not at horse or cart—
my auto runs away down the drive! Bag
hits the grass. I'm on the run, footfalls light
and fleet, though not enough; car comes to light
amid a web of barbed wire. All the books
are unmixed—I see to that bag by bag.
My patron friends, eyebrows up, watch me while
around the car I crawl, snip, collect, cart
away the snare. With mirror broken when
it swiped a fence post, scattered scratches when
it lunged the wire, a crack in the tail light,
my car is a sad sight. "A horse and cart
may thus so go astray, as do the books
the *Kinder* take to the fields," they say. I while
away the time, not anxious yet to bag

the trophy at the library for bag-
to-back route accidents. For surely when
co-worker friends hear this, they'll laugh a while.
But I about the mishap will make light,
for their world is made larger by these books.
Through library doors I trail my red cart;
each bag holds books consumed by minds alight,
and when time, I will once again choose books
that might beguile mind, wile heart, from my cart.

Recipe Box

*My brown wooden file holds a life
of tattered, kitchen-soiled 3x5s:*

Brown-sugar coconut topped Oatmeal Cake
retired from the middle school home ec contest
after winning three years in a row, written
in my mother's school-teacher cursive.

Grandma's German Dills & Gherkins,
seven sweets & sours at holiday dinners.

Christmas Sugars & Wagon Wheels,
in a younger sister's green-inked calligraphy.

A high-school best friend's never-used Nacho Recipe,
lost like she was, for over fifteen years.

Clove & nutmeg perfumed Pumpkin Bread,
in a younger brother's then-round script.

Chinese marinade Shiska-Bobs roasted
over a wood fire in a South Dakota warming house,
after a full-moon night of cross-country skiing.

The reinvented in-law family secret
Chili Sauce, ground just right, typed.

From the hundred-year flooded Mississippi,
Wisconsin Beer Batter for fresh-caught fish.

Indian Curry in Buffalo from my cardamom-scented
walking partner, in her British-schooled hand.

Almond Biscotti translated into English measurements
by a first-generation Italian mother of three in Ohio.

Eucharistic Bread given in Communion
by hard-praying Rhode Island women,
who gifted me with much more
than a hand-flung pottery batter bowl.

Daily Drag

Meet my personal trainer, Casey,
chocolate-and-white spaniel,
brownie mask, freckle face-y.

Her dance of delight at the door,
impossible to resist, she
begs for one stroll, more.

Across the school yard, vacant lot,
around the church-turned-gym,
through the cemetery, we trot.

Flappy eared dog-in-motion,
bobs and weaves, leads
ten-minute-mile in-tow commotion.

For a mile—more, if her way—
I huff and puff, watch,
ponder, compose, or pray.

Observers look askance, say,
"Your dog, it doesn't obey?"
I smile, shrug, look away.

With Casey's tail-wagging glee,
I'll someday greet exercise, maybe.
for now, she springs my lethargy.

Thirst

As enclosed in warmth, you nursed,
My arms, a constant cradle, did sway,
You never seemed to quench your thirst.

My son, when into this world you burst,
We wanted all your fears to allay,
As enclosed in warmth, you nursed.

Though we wished you ignorant of the worst
That this hard world could convey,
You never seemed to quench your thirst.

We wished you to know love's light first,
For joy heavier than grief to always weigh,
As enclosed in warmth, you nursed.

Too soon in the world's ways you'd be versed,
Your growing up we'd not be able to delay—
You never seemed to quench your thirst.

Your rosebud mouth against me pursed,
We rocked peaceful moments away.
As enclosed in warmth, you nursed,
You never seemed to quench your thirst.

Re: ER

From the kitchen window
I saw it happen,
a quick slip—
of serrated metal blade.

I heard you curse,
saw you gather yourself
into a wrinkled brow, taut jaw,
blue eyes dulled to pewter.

Behind the wheel,
on the way to the ER,
I thought, how odd,
to see you in left profile

for wherever we travel,
I'm always the passenger.
You are the comforter,
I, the comforted.

You have clasped me to you,
during births and deaths:
when weeping into the mask,
I despaired at our son's birth,

when curled in fetal position,
I bled out pain of Dad's death,
when bolting from the clinic,
I nearly sacrificed my rebirth.

During this tense ride—
rehearsed roles reversed—
you held your toweled hand,
I, only the steering wheel.

As I delivered you, my patient
passenger, I watched you lumber
through automatic glass doors,
my arms hanging empty.

Autopsy Retort

Though he died eleven years ago,
my father haunts my thoughts; grief
is cyclical, they say (who is "they" anyway?).
Maybe so, yet after all these years,
I didn't expect to be this tearful.

I spent the weekend rummaging
moving boxes for his autopsy report.
The mystery of his death compels
me to seek, if not the why, the how.

Finally reading the autopsy report,
I learn facts about my father
no daughter should ever know.

Amateur of corporeal jigsaw puzzles,
the forensic pathologist tried to measure
the essences of a man: *brain: 1600 grams*
spleen: 300 grams, left kidney: 250 grams
right kidney: 230 grams, right lung: 680 grams
left lung: 550 grams, heart: 490 grams

Yet these numbers ill describe my father.
I will not leave him slabbed, locked
in a cabinet like currency in a vault.
The doctor wrote, "Heart: 490 grams,"
but I know this figure to be false, for

I have seen his tough heart far heavier
as he gazed upon his comatose first-born,
as he struggled in a second-choice career,
as he tried to embrace his father—
stubborn German—and was rebuffed.

I have seen his delicate heart lighter, too,
when he and my mother shared secret smiles,
when he celebrated our grades, trophies, medals,
when he and I waltzed on my wedding day.

Though I learn figures about my father
I never desired to know,
this reverse alchemist never knew
any father figures that were true.

Wild Must Be Wild

    —after *Depression in Winter,* by Jane Kenyon

There comes a little space
    between the south side of the boulder
        and the perennial garden
just right for the rabbit burrow
I found that spring: kittens
the size of Easter eggs almost
ready to wean and run—
or freeze, in hopes the hawk is blind.

My daughter scooped one up,
    carried it around in her hoodie,
        like her own Velveteen Rabbit,
until I told her: *wild must be wild.*
I prayed there be no traffic
as the kittens scattered ahead of us
across the road to the woods.

I opened my eyes to waving grasses
    and sighed.

Into Blue

I hover over my father's shoulder as he exits the highway. His face clenches in pain. He leaves open the door of his red pickup. He collapses in the restaurant entrance. When the EMTs arrive, they find his heart stopped.

After the funeral, I spy the note on the telephone stand: *Hal died of a heart attack*, written in blue ballpoint in Mom's hand. My throat closes, stomach lurches. I slip the note into my jeans pocket. Later I eat it.

I taste blood. My mouth hurts. Opens wide. A zero. Null. My tongue works my teeth. Wiggles them. Starting with the smile, my teeth drop out, fall into my hand. I try to shove them back in place, but they won't stay.

In the perennial border, the butterfly bush hosts a late monarch and hummingbird moth. Together. I lie prone back on the grass. The moth disappears into the asparagus foliage. The monarch flutters upward. Over the stockade fence, into blue. Vanishes.

I fly over the high hills, over alpine terrain. My flapping arms lift me ever higher. Until I reach the rocky peak summit in the thin, bright light blue cold crispness. I strain . . . fold inward . . . fall . . . wake before I hit the ground. Heart crashing in my ears.

Paradigm Shift

Unformed hips hugged

        by a black rubber seat,

          she grasped chains, complaining

in rhythm to the swing's pitch,

at arc's end tilted back,

        stepped on the clouds,

          swept the ground with her hair.

    Knobby knees, bruised shins hidden

              under knee socks, feet saddled in shoes

    propelled her upward with each breath,

as if she could have vaulted the bars

        holding her (s)wings to earth—

                merged with her lighter self.
When the gears of motion ratcheted,

        the world lost its center,

        shifted from the nest of surety

into the fear fall of doubt.

Heart in My Garden

I stomp, turn over shovels
full in, of hot anger,
heavy hard-hearted clay.

Becky's not my daughter,
but she could be,
prematurely wise playmate.

Is she meant to slip away
like dry sand through fingers,
clutching at hope?

Cancer doesn't care
she loves family, music,
sun on her face.

I unearth pottery shards,
today only junk finds,
not mosaic-maker's jewels.

Radiation, chemo, surgery,
Dr. So-and-So's alternative—
they're all the same.

Glint of silver draws me.
Between fingers and thumb,
I grasp a thin heart pendant.

I rub away dark clay,
find *Love* engraved in script,
know her future is near.

3:30 a.m.

    —in memory of R.D.

That she would fly from us we had long feared.
When I saw her pale face subdued, dark eyes
glazed with morphine, I knew that her time neared:

Like a Luna moth, she would realize
she must pierce chrysalis, emerge, unfold
silken wings, false eyes, pixelated scales.

That August hot afternoon I consoled
my heart sore daughter while within me gales
of disbelief, denial raged unchecked.

From restless sleep that night I sprang awake
to her screams—headache, dreams of life wrecked.
Soon we knew what tenor that day would take:

She had flitted translucid past the moon,
lit, danced for us to *the* celestial tune.

Mid-January Snow

thread-bare blanket of ice
        could not   efface even the fallen
soapstone grave markers.

          Sharp wind snatched their words,
as piling from vans, cars,   the mothers pointed
      third-graders bundled in winter-wear
toward the guest of honor, resting
            under mounded *soul*, a greenery wreath.
On notes held hard   against each other's backs,
     her once-classmates scribbled
hopes, missives, secret wishes, tied
        them to ribbony balloon tails.

     Shouting the birthday song,
they released them.   Balloons,
     purple and pink—her favorite colors.
Biting chapped lips, they watched
         as the wind swept them upward,
like soap bubbles   chased by butterflies.
Over a barnside grove of diseased elms,
         stretching   toward the clouds.

Analogies

::

life : butterfly

live : life :: create : creation

self : source :: subconscious : spring
spring : fall :: youth : maturity

make : destroy :: cry : laughter
laughter : light :: water : buoy

love : pain :: salve : burn
burn : fire :: pain : love

horror : wonder :: scream : silence
silence : mutism :: tunnel vision : blindness

past : memory :: future : vision
vision : sight :: imagination : mind

art : world :: butterfly : wind

::

repository : heart

repose : repository :: live : life

ache : pain :: happiness : joy
joy : tears :: sorrow : tears

affinity : union :: conflict : rupture
rupture : reconcile :: age : renew

beauty : soulfulness :: skin : flesh
flesh : blood :: mind : thought

happiness : smile :: sadness : frown
frown : smile :: despair : hope

mindfulness : now :: memory : past
past : future :: sheer : opaque

urn : ashes :: my heart : vanished things

Lot

At noon and 6 p.m. the cathedral bells sound, call to travelers
and loiterers free from time otherwise: no watches, no cellphones.

Dogs of all sizes and colors, long-haired and short, lead
their people down the sidewalk, sniff and squat.

Black-robed nuns at the convent next door cross the parking lot,
while nearby a flock of starlings looks on from a tall elm.

Cars line up in the lot to take turns at the food distribution table.
Curbside pickup.

In silence, falling snow dances under parking lot spotlights.

An SUV and car drive up from opposite directions and pause
under the covered drop-off. Hands reach out from windows
and make a quick exchange.

The three-million-dollar renovation brings truckloads of construction
workers, waiting to start their days.

Neighbors dress in the dark,
then turn on the lights.

Dozens of chairs and tables from the basement social hall
assemble in the lot. Cars and trucks pull up, and the tangle
of taking discards off to new owners unwinds.

The thunderstorm roar of the helicopter as it passes low overhead
toward the hospital helipad pauses conversations, elicits prayers
for those in flight, maybe.

Decked out groomsmen gather outside until the appointed hour.
Enter. The party bus patiently waits.

State police raid the bishop's residence next to the cathedral.
After a new bishop arrives, no more nasty notes appear
on apartment dwellers' cars parked in the wrong lot.

Covid outdoor Mass with parishioners in their cars spaced out
in the parking lot looks like a drive through. Even Communion
is delivered car side. Music is not optional.
Neighbors start when funeral salute shots ring out.
Gunfire, no matter what kind, attracts attention in this quarter.

Chattering children and mothers or keepers have a play date
at the back of the lot. They ride trikes and color with chalk,
argue over a baby doll.

One morning a young boy in a green t-shirt and shorts runs
out from the church. He splashes in the fresh puddles
until a woman grabs his waving arms and herds him
toward an SUV, ends his unbridled baptism.

Hydrology of Tears

From an ancient subterranean reservoir,
(aquifer of the limbic "lizard brain"),
lacrimal lake in a body made of water,

springs laced with minerals flow,
form rivulets, then tributaries of silk
on the delta, salt on the tongue,

speak the inarticulable, release
the geyser-like pressure of life—
prove our fragile humanity.

Tether's End

Spying the lone goose high overhead, she stretches to tether's end, leaps—
lands, understanding in a sniff the unreachable nature of her desire.
Why should a spaniel bred to follow invisible scents spring heavenward?

Roaming the boundaries of her domain, she chases flitting shadows,
unseen trails, meanders only made visible to my dulled senses
by the first snow, sprinkled like holy water on a crowd.

Dresden Plate

Holidays we crowd our mother's house:
aunts, uncles, nieces, nephews
finding favorite relatives, siblings, spouses,
playing games, watching sports,
eating, drinking, doing dishes,
talking, listening long into the night,
sleeping wherever we will—
on foldout beds, sleeping bags, and
mattresses pulled from under beds;
lying shoulder to shoulder
in my mother's bed, I listen
to her gentle, metronomic breathing,
sense weight, the Dresden Plate,
flannel bat heating me in a steady
rhythm of stitches joining years,
cotton floss embroidering lives:
Grandma and her mother had measured,
cut, pieced greens, grays, blues, browns
in a dozen empty plates atop a table.
Around the quilt's bound borders
they sewed a double helix, tiny
repeating stitches that bind us all.

Mousery

Mind on task's demand,
not what I might find in hand

where my cotton gloves nested,
on the garden shed shelf,

when tawny micelets, wingless bats

flew, flailing, clinging air, my hair,
shoulders, neck, both bare.

Their timorous squeaks,
my astonished shrieks mingled

as I slap-danced about the shed,

realized I'd just done what
I'd said I would never do:

become unglued by creatures
modest in size, who imply held the trump:

surprise.

False Crocus Geometer

My head pinned to the sheet,
a moth framed by vertigo
on a Victorian bed of milkweed silk.
No fluttering; only stillness
lest the world resume its tilted course;
only silence, thoughts flitting
from peony to rose.

Bruised, Not Broken

Runaway corner cupboard
turns tables on my thumb,
crashed between door and jamb.

Subcutaneous ecchymosis thrives,
drives my hand among frozen cubes,
numbs enough the signal thumb.

I steer this white-knuckle journey
down middle-of-the-life road,
past *carrefours* of cares, vowing

not to retrace that costly route
through black-and-blue depressions:
potholes, kitchen sinkholes once
drained me of life until numb.

When I shelved my "lack of boundaries"
among capsule bottles
and beloved bodies,
psychosis arrived at a cul-de-sac.

Now, as then, my compass—
solely bruised, not broken—
its nacreous nail under pain
clotted, rewarms by degrees.

Window Washer

My husband hates to wash windows.
Our longtime joke—we'll move again
before it's time to wash them. So,

nose-burning bucket of ammonia water
in one hand, squeegee in the other,
tired old tee-shirts draped over my arm,
I survey this anti-archival chore.

The sliding glass door presents its evidence:
fingerprints, spaniel drool and nose prints,
windblown dust, a feather pasted with blood.

I wet, wipe, squeegee, dry edges, corners,
glide open the door, cross the track, repeat.
Door open, I stand astride, tilting my head
left, right, to see what remains: a film,

echoes of an interior|exterior viewpoint,
like those black-and-white drawings—
are they vases or faces? we ask ourselves.

My Perfect Cup of Coffee

is not the plastic travel mug
of Breakfast Blend that topples

from the center car console
onto my khaki slacks,

not Columbian or French Roast,

not afternoon cappuccino
with a hazelnut shot,

not Café JoJo's mocha latte
iced with whipped cream,

not keep-me-awake caffeine
microwaved four times bitter.

My perfect cup is home perked,
sweetened with sugar and cream:

when my love smiles at me,
that liquid look in his dark eyes,

and I want to cup his smooth cheeks
in my hands—

sip, drink, gulp
until the pot runs dry.

Picky Eater

— an erasure of three shorts from *Cook's Illustrated*

Why We [Cook]

the most basic
    nourishment
the very beginning
our love,   care

to fashion   a set
that is

better
          solace and
   comfort
in difficult times.

[July & Aug., 2017, p. 1]

[Joy in] the Journey

  moving
          people
   always traveling
  migrating
       leave their
homes behind,

      Come with
  them   time

cherish   previous lives
                      emblematic
      their new home
         embodying the
soul   seen from a
longer perspective
  startling

[Sept. & Oct. 2017, p. 1]

The Benefits of Being Dull

                    dull and matte from
years of use   Lucky
you.   put
new sheets   in the test
     times weren't getting the job done.
            pallid and limp,   but—
       emerged from the
past, we
absorb and transfer   more efficiently

you should celebrate, not mourn.

[Oct. 2018, p. 31]

Tonic

If you should grow root
bound—static, wilted, pale—
I will repot you.

Burrowing to your taproot,
I will grasp it
providently, transfer it to new loam
(fertile, soft, moist) inside
a cache-potted container,
ornamented in mosaic,
your rearranged life-shards.

In my sunlight and shade,
I will restore your turgor,
tease fresh shoots from you.

Hardware

A trio of older men, two gray, one bald, looks up as we approach the counter. The phone rings and on the left *hello, parts department. What can I do for ya today.* We're there to hand over a pair of lawn tractor mower blades for sharpening and to buy a backup pair to use now. *Guys, he wants an electric repair. Do we still do that? No, not if he didn't buy it here. Tell him he'll have to go online and contact the maker.* I'm tagging along in part for the nostalgia of a hardware that repairs and has parts in bins so if you only want a single screw or washer, you can buy just that. *Hello, you still there? We can't fix that here . . . call . . .* Our guy finds blades on the stock shelves and puts them on the counter in front of us. Covered in what seems to be the thick green paint of up north cabins, they don't look sharp enough to cut a single blade of grass. *Don't go at 'em all angry. Be polite first. Then if you hafta, be an ass. You know that old saying, you can catch more flies with honey . . .* When we ask, we learn these blades are covered with a protective coating that'll come off after a couple minutes of resistance. They'll soon be as sharp as razors.

Signs of Character

I hear my voice as if far away,
muffled, like gauze held over a wound,
reading aloud about a creature
whose slashing claws threaten,
as drugged, you doze on the bed,
awaiting the plastic surgeon's arrival.

I cannot know you just hear murmurs,
not the gory tale you chose prompting
my hate for this novel and author.

It is no matter of survival—but beauty,
your lightning smile deformed.
I see again when beyond my reach,
you and Casey went mouth to muzzle
over a blanket, a tug-of-toy,
canines closing on your soft, pursed lips.

I cannot know your slow-motion thoughts,
your shocked realization of torn flesh,
as your hand covered a delayed scream.

When the surgeon arrives, he greets you;
saying, "I can fix that," he does so,
with deft sutures I refuse to count,
knowing mothers will question, "How many?"
Later I serve ice cream, Darvocet,
hear echoes, "I'd get rid of *that dog* . . ."

I cannot know that you will dry tears,
christen the scars signs of character,
be the first to accept, to forgive.

At the Y

 —September 11, 2001

Watching from the lifeguard chair,
I see caps contain their ponytails—
not their exuberance—as noses
clipped by rubber, they slip
from the pool deck into liquid music:
signets winging low on/in/under water.

Treading side by side, they dance,
smile playfully slap the water,
lay out—legs splayed, arms fluttering—
become a momentary water lily,
then snap shut like an oyster,
submerging fingers to toes.

Seconds later two right legs thrust up
from the water—pointed ballet toes
like swans looking heavenward—
rotate in complete circles, finally
sink in slow motion out of sight.

Heave

I lie next to you on the bed
propped up with pillows,
you languid, leaning against me,
we in shorts and tees—sticky
                you reek of cigarettes and rum.
You mumble, I should've (stopped her)
could die (too).

Sobs and retches interrupt
the hours—I hold you, my right
arm on your bony shoulder,
my left tries to circle your thin waist.
                You turn away from me, dry heave,
confess to a trio of tattoos
you hadn't yet acknowledged
but that I'd glimpsed one day
when your tee rose with your arms.

A heave and a whiff of sour stomach
                collapse 18 years to 8 months.

My baby daughter then, when
a simple virus caused the void,
                then the emptiness a new hunger
time and again, you in distress,
I vigilant
as we lay the night on towels
spread out on the carpeted floor.

World in Motion

My daughter, frantic in the midnight, wakes me to drive her,
holds the texted suicide note phone in her hand.

In the ER waiting room, the father cries, tells how he had tried
to hold her up, call 911. He curses the boyfriend who'd broken
up with her from the Army by text, threatens to kill him.

The divorced parents talk of their daughter's manic-depression—
maybe she'd be luckier not to live.

My yellow hoodie shrouds my face somewhat protects
my neck from hospital cold as stress clenches every muscle.

The thin hand on the Pegasus clock ticks 360 degrees,
a mechanical pulse measuring seconds as the night creeps by.

A van pulls up to the ER drop off. A man hops out, leaves
the door gaping. He runs through the ER doors, returns
to the passenger side with a wheel chair, rushes his laboring wife
past me, as a nurse instructs: take that elevator to the
maternity wing.

By the security office door sits a box labeled *human organs*.
Printed on the side are icons for body parts—one of them eyes.

We wait hours for a specialist. My daughter sits in the parking lot
with the other best friend she hadn't seen earlier that night.

A pair of rabbits frolics on the lawn near the hospital entrance.

The specialist comes and goes. My daughter and her friend trail
a nurse through ER doors, are allowed to say good-bye before—

The dark granite boulder at the visitor entrance is meant to revolve
when water flows beneath it. As the morning shift arrives,
a custodian turns on the water, setting the world in motion.

Bear-Garden

> By modern morality, the sport of bear-baiting
> is a repugnant form of blood sport.

Welcome to the bear-garden, where chained
to the post in the middle of the ring,
the black bear sow, young yet scarred,
growls, snarls, lunges at her tormentors:
dogs of all breeds, trained by litter mates, bitches,
and circumstances to prey on any weakness.
In the gallery spectators place bets,
cast knowing looks, make rude gestures
at the moving target, who would gouge flesh
if not held in check by iron rings.
At the back of the room a student chimes,
"Last year, I made a sub cry."

Personal Pompeii

I spark wild fires with my husband,
      children, friends—myself,

smash the clay vase, in mid-day
      burrow under the comforter,

pretending I can't feel
      in the dark, red-hot cinders,
           needing only a breath
                  to flame.

Some inner force floods my psyche,
      scalding invective incinerates me,

like lava over unsuspecting Pompeii.
      I can't tamp this vicious stream,

yet, perhaps it will spew so fast,
      archaeologists may someday un(re)-
           cover my cerebral remains,
                  intact.

I Believe in Silence (of a sort)

I believe in silence:
not the kind that is shamed upon you,
not the fingers around the throat,
not the suffocating lack of breath,
not the look that paralyzes.

Silence speaks its own language:
between the words,
between the lines,
between one pair of eyes
and another pair.

Silence explains change
for it is in the quiet of minds
and hearts that we can hear
beyond the din of glitch-filled modern life.
We can understand and imagine,
then make real.

My thoughts move/are atoms moved.
Until my fingers work
or vocal cords vibrate,
the interior words are silent:
impotent, harmless
to all but myself.

I choose silence
to safeguard myself and others.
If the words I want most to say are lodged
in my throat while tears
stream down my face,

this is so because: I
am a coward, or thoughtful,
or a combination of both.
A mime.

I must be sure of my words;
once I break silence
there is no turning back.
Unlike words written on paper,
paper that can be crumpled and thrown
away, spoken words ride
on the wind and into ears.

Spoken words disturb the universe
because they've left the speaker's mouth.
Even if no one hears these words,
the speaker knows she
he whispered them or spoke
them or sang
them, or cried
them, or spat
them or howled them.

Technology works against silence.
It multi-tasks in our faces,
our ears,
our minds.

In a whirl of digital cacophony,
it dissipates our thoughts to
static until we become numb and foolish.

Nor does it let us
crumple up the paper or
retrieve the unsent email
or text message from the post box,
the suicide note
from the recipient's cellphone—too late.

No matter how many times
someone says *I'm sorry*,
the damage wrought
by words on the wind
is already done.

Better to guard silence.

Declaration

Heavy with the weight of escorting guests to you
in the side chapel before the Mass of Resurrection,
I escaped to the memorial rose garden at the entrance.

Bright in the October sun, the last roses fueled
the clustered monarchs for their southward journey.

These super-sized monarchs would not
be those returning the next spring.
How will their descendants know the way?

The only choices they have: trust the process,
or be carried along on the winds regardless.

I returned to the chapel and your empty chrysalis.
My children, your grandchildren, gathered around me.

"We'll remember you in the rising and setting sun,"
I declared to your face a final time,
"and in the flutter of monarchs' wings."

Some Things Shift

    —after *The Hours* by Michael Cunningham

When you handed me your copy of *The Hours*,
I didn't know then it was a setup.
You just said the writing was beautiful,
you knew that I'd read some Virginia Woolf—
though not *Mrs. Dalloway*—you knew
I was struggling in my marriage.

Propped up on pillows alone in bed,
that week I read the novel;
it was lyrical, but its plots pained me,
especially the young boy
who made his mother into a monster
for life—for leaving to save herself.
For not realizing she couldn't survive
if she'd stayed.

One morning as I lay in bed with eyes closed,
my snoring husband next to me,
I felt surface from deep inside
the silent scream: *I want a divorce.*

Later I texted you for your whereabouts.
Starbucks. I found you there,
with your usual French press. You rose
to greet me, in the middle
of the coffee shop, held me
as I sobbed.

Eventually we had coffee.
Eventually I filed for divorce.
Eventually my son forgave me
for not taking him with me.

Years later when I told you
for a moment that day
I'd felt ambushed, you explained:
Once someone gave you *The Hours*,
that it had righted your course,
that you have to decide
to stay in that time of unhappiness
or be brave enough to start over.

Geodes

1

In a whorl of concentric circles,
    grows sugar beet, pale,
      sweet cousin of borsch;
       immersed in soil,
        it taps the
         roots of
          con
          scious
             ness,

2

while disingenuous geode,
    inorganic doppelganger,
        poem unto itself
            (crystalline introspector)
      meshes silicon molecules
    under cataclysmic pressure
into glistening multi-facets,
        heaved upward by contractions—
          heat, frost, tectonic plates
            tossed by the ages
                down mountainsides—
      becomes a Native thunder stone.   O

3

As I dangle my thought's train
  into the potent slurry,
    grain
    by
    pane
    poems
    granually
    emerge,
    form
    a
    rock
    candy
    necklace,
    redolent
    of
    my
    super
    saturated
    life.

Final Proof

Fiction's plausibility denies me
truth: I ponder events, my life. I know
the critic might deny the strangest though
true-life tale, say "impossible." Maybe.

Events, converging webs wherever we
stand—mystery magnified on high or low,
minute or large, then and now, to and fro—
declare there to be more than we can see.

For every person transactions are made,
patterns spun—unknown code—and nature
or nurture conspire with this world. Aloof,
they plot unseen courses until when laid

out over time, the facts emerge, ensure
at last: history is the final proof.

About the Author

JEANNE BLUM LESINSKI graduated from DePauw University with a BA in French. While raising her three children, she worked variously as a freelance writer and editor for nonfiction publishers, a home service librarian to the Amish, and a teaching assistant in developmental English at a community college. She wrote the best-selling juvenile biography of Microsoft founder Bill Gates for A&E books and did research and translation work for the hybrid film *Poe (and the Museum of Lost Arts)* by MiShinnah Productions. Lesinski's poetry and creative nonfiction have appeared in journals and anthologies, including *Ginosko Vol. 2*, *Poem, Revised*, and *Among the Happy Poets* (Theodore Roethke Society). Her recent work has appeared online and in print publications, among others, *The Dunes Review*, *Midway Journal*, and *Plainsongs*. Her haibun "Embroidery" was a finalist in *The Ekphrastic Review* Women Artists contest. When not at her computer she might be found in a garden or on a bike trail.

Shanti Arts

Nature · Art · Spirit

Please visit us online
to browse our entire book catalog,
including poetry collections and fiction,
books on travel, nature, healing, art,
photography, and more.

Also take a look at our highly regarded art
and literary journal, *Still Point Arts Quarterly*,
which may be downloaded for free.

www.shantiarts.com

www.ingramcontent.com/pod-product-compliance
Lightning Source LLC
LaVergne TN
LVHW041346080426
835512LV00006B/640